Tempo

Also by Sarah Day

Tempo

Sarah Day

PUNCHER & WATTMANN

First published in 2013
Published by Puncher and Wattmann
PO Box 441
Glebe NSW 2037
http://www.puncherandwattmann.com
puncherandwattmann@bigpond.com

National Library of Australia
Cataloguing-in-Publication entry:

Day, Sarah
Tempo

ISBNs (paperback) 9781922186379 (e-book) 9781922186355 (kindle) 9781922186362

I. Title.
A821.3

Cover design by Matthew Holt
Printed by McPhersons Printing Group

This project has been assisted by the Australian Government through the Australia Council, its arts funding

Australian Government

Australia | **Council**
for the Arts

for Andrea

Contents

A present of things past, a present of things present,
a present of things future … what then is time? If no one asks of me,
I know; if I wish to explain to him who asks, I know not
         – St Augustine

… the so-called imaginary time is really the real time,
and what we call real time is just a figment of our imaginations.
         – Stephen Hawking

El Iskandariya

When marsh birds pooled out of the sky like ink
on water to devour the barley flour
that Alexander's men had laid to mark
the mythic city's boundaries, the hour

seemed lost beyond recall: the city's walls;
to north and south, the marvellous Gates of Moon
and Sun; and from across a vast expanse
of sea, Elysian winds to cool the streets— all gone

as ominous flocks eclipsed the light; lost too
the traffic of ideas from the known world
to those deep harbours, Mareotis filled
replete with shimmering waters from the Nile.

In the flurry of wing and hungry beak
though, the soothsayers saw no travesty
but a message in the darkened air
the future city would be blessed with plenty.

New Year's Eve

We're back at the beginning once again
— a bus loop or a joy-ride at the fair —
on our centrifugal journey round the sun,
this time and distance that we call a year.

No fixed stars or celestial dome,
our solar system's not the bell-jar home
it used to be; we're on a limb in space,
an orrery upon a mantelpiece.

From Earth, this tireless spinning orb that laps
at sixty-seven thousand miles per hour,
we do not seem to move at all; we are
like passengers in flight, woolgatherers ...

A view from elsewhere in our galaxy
could show how we appear from the outside,
might illustrate the poignancy —
that we're all in this together for the ride,

as round about the sun we go again
like travellers that don't get off the train.

In Time, Pompeii

Here, the cast of a dead dog
looking like a modern de Bruyckere
caught in the knowing instant
inside the sprung coil of its spine
narrow paws crossed front and back,
guileless and devout,
two millennia tumbling from its open mouth.
For contrast, here's comely Eros
with his vulval conch, or
Venus standing on one leg
raising her great, workaday foot.
The cast of the young woman
is forever that — a young woman,
supine, elbows bent, weeping
into her hands. Alone,
like the mule-driver crouched
and also weeping into his hands, shrinking,
from whatever terror lies before him.

The indiscriminate moment
surrendered through time:
this is how it was that hour,
life's day to day miscellany —
the mule-driver's mind on his load,
his sacks of flour or rolls of cloth.
Now, as then,
Cupid rides a crab and parrots dine with doves.

Telephus sups on the teat of the doe
who curves her neck to watch
and licks his thigh.

Through ancient brick-kerbed streets
along colonnade ellipses,
past Apollo's Temple to where roads,
houses, shops are gently consumed
by living earth.
Here is a wall, emerging and vanishing
into soil like the words of a poem
inscribed in stone from millennia past.
What more might be revealed?
I might, with clawed fingers, dig
to see if perimeters exist at all
but walk instead upon
the brief gradient that leads
through time to a ploughed field
where a man with a hoe works,
meditative, desultory.
Like the mule-driver and the young woman
or the stories on the mosaic walls,
he is not from my century either.
He will not meet my eye
as I skirt his tilled boundary to the station,
await the crowded train
with its noisy freight of twentieth century
passengers bound for Naples.

Northern Window

The chill dawn of midwinter;
a morning in which day will never break.
Spires and cranes emerge from vapour,
a streetlamp casts a reflection that adheres
like Byzantine gold leaf to the water of the canal.
The breeze sets it rippling into an epiphany
through which a coot – how does she bear
the subzero cold? – crosses and recrosses
as if to absorb some of the miracle of light
this day in which there will be none.
On the furthest bank, people on black bicycles
– no hats, no gloves – push down on pedals as if
 there were only one speed at this time of day,
in this weather – neither fast, nor slow.
Soon the crane driver will climb
the scaffolding to his post suspended
above the grey city of Amsterdam
and the boom will commence its slow
geometry of arcs in an open-armed gesture
as if to say "See, see, all of this".
Scenes of pilgrims in mosaic
leach into focus on the high brick walls
of the Rijksmuseum as the carillon
in the slate towers chimes its fairy-tale tune
to announce that morning has begun
though no awakening of light affirms this;
the streetlamps, at a signal,
become recalcitrant and in the canal waters
dwindle to prosaic yellow spots

before giving way entirely
to sombre, liquid forms of winter trees.

On the sill, the Venezuelan statue of Mary
turns her back to the window,
unmoved, disturbed perhaps
by Anglo-Saxon melancholy, interiority;
she fingers the pearls of her rosary,
looks, with insouciance,
away from the grey northern dawn
to the open blue skies of Latin America
where the fishermen's wives cast
her many likenesses in terra cotta.
Like the glittering gold
on the canal, the pearls on her crown
and gown breathe brilliant evanescence.

Afterimage

The image lit against the eye's dark lid
is often clearer than the light of day.
Sometimes I see the view amended:

the missing key, the winter tree inverted
as a photo negative. a blazing x-ray
of the image lit against the eye's dark lid.

In conversation, details that were hid
may come to light in such or such a way
(for better or for worse) the view's amended.

It shows what's dimmed and what's illuminated,
the shifting chiaroscuro. Who's to say
the image lit against the eye's dark lid

is closer/further from the one intended?
And what directs the cutting room, the replay
– where sometimes the truth can be amended?

With luck, by second chance I'm visited
by definition in a field of grey;
in the image lit against the eye's dark lid,
I sometimes see the view amended.

River Fisher

Against the cool push and shove
of the river's current, keep walking;
a gum tree beetle might be hatching
this clear morning that opens up water
like a lens; across the taut surface
wind might blow the eggs of a cadis moth.
In flowing water, still ponds reside:
a trout, suspended in a boulder's vacuum
might watch a line of bubbles
slip downstream like an elver.
Water hugs the lungs like apprehension,
resists an interloper, insists on its own way,
would upend you from a slippery stone
and keep right on going.

Mower

Eternity's the green concentric lines:
today's, last spring's and all of those before,
continuous as ancestral memory;
the paddock's slow transition from deep green
to lighter pale, the texture of the stubbled stalks,
the even parallels of altered hues.
Truck, mower, circling in a pas de deux,
cut grass pouring like water from a hose.

This blade against the grass is present time,
frogs and rabbits leaping from the wheel,
tall grass wilting as it falls away
all slipshod into windrows,
the arrow of a hawk's decent
shadow of the moment's measurement.

Plantation

Like Huxley's brave new world these trees
breathe death in life. The regiment
of parallels sequesters dark.
No birds sing in the precincts of
its dreary avenues. The canopy's
bereft. In the absence of underbrush,
mercenary brambles have
unrolled their mess of barbs. Insects
have taken leave. The wind is stilled.
A single wire delineates
this cold spiked parcel of hush from
the cropped field with its remnant gum,
survivor of a former time
that's reached its solitary prime;
a tree of life, host to whistlers,
the tintinnabulum of green
rosellas, and, at dusk, upon
its eminence, the inky-black
acuity of forest ravens.

Seed Vault of Longyearbyen

The pharaohs would have understood
the need to circumvent the afterlife:
a single entrance/exit in the desert sands/
the permafrost; discretion's art to hide

a subterranean corridor to
futures horizontal to the gradient.
Like lapis pomegranate, lotus fruit
and gilded rows of ankh, hieroglyphs of life,

the endless shelves of dormant DNA
beguile the flux of time or chance or sense.
A vault outside a town upon
an island in an archipelago

close to the Pole encoding icily
the arcane seed of rice and wheat
and broccoli: subliminal beginnings in
this mausoleum to the Afterwards.

The Raven's Bill

rests its case
at the foot of the wood-heap.
Clamped shut
on slow laconic vowels,
the beak with its clean know-how
minus the bird.
Maggot and ant
have conspired like analysts,
scoured right back
to corvid truculence.
Polished, sagacious
as a sonnet
or a sacred law,
steel-cast to flay carrion,
pierce tempests;
a diamond-cutter
match for any oyster shell's
insouciance and the careless
and mercenary world;
this obsidian bill,
defiant on the palm
as fortitude, resistance.

Lightning in a Portuguese Garden

The garden, lit up in a realm that's not the day's,
flickers in an instant outside time.
Vision's metallic on the tongue

as thunder rattles in its tin somewhere
over the Atlantic, then ricochets to here and now.
A pepper tree's electric replica,

the afterimage of a sculpted hedge,
ghosts of olive, oleander,
everything a likeness to itself,

bogus and more real,
in this blinding light that's not the sun's,
inimical to night's taboo.

The elements are all the same
yet wanting weight and mass: on the table
summer's empty gourds are lit within;

a net from some abandoned game
of shuttlecock drifts numinous
in the vacuum of the approaching storm.

Dark's charged.
Before the light goes out
the limestone wall's ephemeral.
Night discloses more than day.

Glover in Paradise

1. First Impressions

Just what the perspicuity of trees
implied, he wasn't sure but let his hand
sketch out the pendant foliage
while eyes, half shut, observed the purpling
undulation into distance through
its flickering blue lucidity. Candid
light affirmed in this utopia
a leaning towards frankness; Europe's
umbra lay a five months sail away
from this all-seeing avatar, the noonday sun
which lit up scruffy non-conformity
as blithe convention. He resolved to read
the spaces rather than
the salient features of this foreign land.

2. Palinode

With failing eyesight he began to see
there had been flaws in Paradise,
that in the arcane language of the bush
and plain, an absence figured, prominent
as man-fern, eucalypt and fallen tombs
of trunks; ubiquitous as cloud-strewn blue;
it was tacit in the ancient skylines.
Another world from Houghton-on-the-Hill,
the southern idyll he'd inhabited
was gone, indeed, had never been, except
in his entranced imagination.
The mix where two worlds met was all trompe l'oeil.
Every place he looked on now became
a scene of loss and scene of shame.

3. Camera Lucida

As if erasing every autograph
and every painted layer of his life,
he peeled back Europe's blackened foregrounds first,
yellow's lamina of copal varnish
the scorn of the Academy; the voyage;
the palette of Van Diemen's light came last,
in which he'd seen Grace manifest
the olive shades and split-brush tussock grass;
she-oak scrub and thumb print foliage;
right back to chalk and lead-white. Linen's blank
erasure, or beginning. Did he move
backwards or forwards into piety,
the simple chapel in the bush,
the picket fence around the modest tomb?

Notre Dame de la Garde

Marseille

The eye of a needle through which
the earth's curve and the green sea thread,
the gilded mother and her child

might be the first point and the last
to which the sailor's gaze is drawn.
Up close, she seems about to topple from

the dizzying bell tower, a silhouette
against the sky; the church itself
precarious, a crow's nest on

a chalky cliff. Some images
my memory refuses to relinquish ...
like fishing boats suspended on

the cold still air of the basilica,
miniatures of life-sized craft
out on the waves; their nylon threads

a figment of the mind. A fleet
of votive offerings hanging in
a gold-leaf vacuum of calm above

the silent rows of empty pews.
She leans, a falling figurine
towards the port of Joliette,

and sees, in her peripheral view
the ferries come and go to Corsica.

The Mirror

The older children gathered like
diplomats or government ministers
and closed ranks. Then parted ways
on the question of whether to tell.

At the bottom of the *brook*
(this was Upholland, Lancashire)
a large mirror lay face-up in the flood
reflecting two bodies of moving water.

Something spooked, turned us all
on our heels, which may have been
the missing margin between illusion
and substance in the vortices and currents

though we were young enough for this to be
unlikely. There was a mirage of bluebells.
It was still raining. The mystery of how a piece
of furniture got to be among the river stones

was not a burning question. When we ran,
we ran towards and away from a reflection,
a glimpse through bubbles of what we'd come to see
as imminence or constancy in motion.

Shadow Trees

We see but shadowy outlines
                                        — Plato

The shadow trees arrive in handcarts
and on the backs of trucks.
The City Council seems to have
a policy on chiaroscuro:
sylvan stencils on bitumen,
stucco and concrete façade.
Some silhouettes I find I have
always been walking through
like numinous fig leaves on a sandstone wall;
the three-D geometry of banksia in the porch;
a winter oak projected on a public lawn,
twin ashes breathing intricate as lungs
across a busy street.
Whether the light is sharper, I don't know.
Shadow trees become more prominent
year by year, outlined by sun and moon
and streetlamp. We drive through them
on the asphalt in our cars. Like the dead,
they stand among us on the streets,
patterning our hands, our feet and faces.
Like wood and chlorophyll they bend
and reconfigure in the wind.

Alzheimer Ward
For Margaret and Gabriel

Adrift from past and future,
the present moment's an impasse
with which Christ on his alloy cross
above the door perhaps identifies.
Daytime: three chairs arranged to correlate
the distant space between three intimates:
desultory comments tossed into the vacant air
intersecting now and then to make
promiscuous, incoherent sense.
Their landmarks are behind them now,
wartime weddings, youthful wives –
trinkets of lost, forgotten lives.
Sometimes through the maze and melee
in the ordered room they might look up
with limpid eye from tea and sweet biscuits
to ask like the Countess Rosina
where are they, the beautiful moments?
Yet even so, when a face floats, nameless
at the open door
like a hazy memory of love –
something painful like rapture moves the heart.

Skies

I. Twenty-first Century Sky

As one who has risen to meet
most of the dawns in her life
and who knows clouds well
from out-door farming work,
a love of things that grow
and eighty years of looking up
as solace; and who observes closely
before making any sort of pronouncement,
she is someone to pay attention to
when she remarks that skies
are changing. I have been looking
and wondering about this,
though some conclusions defy us.
At 42 degrees south on an island
surrounded by the shifting skies
of oceans, flux is the very nature
of the spaces overhead.
Looking for change when what is constant
is change is harder than it may seem,
and sounds a double negative
that might cancel itself out
like multiplying minuses.
Though there is a lexicon
for what we simply call clouds
we are bereft of words
for the inconstancy of what we live with daily.
Veering towards matter,

perhaps we are less adept at reading motion.
She may be right, skies may be changing;
there's something to be said for being observant.

I'd like to hear from other sky-watchers:
tractor-drivers in the prairies, on the Steppes,
reindeer herdsmen, fishermen
across the seven seas,
people who live on mountains
and in deserts, office-workers
gazing through glass,
their thoughts on transience, and motion
as recorded by clouds.
Are we missing something?
This is a question I think about
and keep looking up to find the answer to.
By way of comparison,
do you recall the skies across your childhood?

II. Meteorology

… From the Greek *raised up, lofty,*
we watch the motions and events of skies.
One way or another
this science absorbs all of us
from office window to the deck
of trawler and fishing tub,
the arctic to the tropics.
Who is not a weather-watcher?
Bird, beast, butterfly
the lizard trickling through a crack in dry rock

to enjoy a cloud's passing from the eye of the sun?
We follow the weather
with the avidity of its indifference to us.
Looking up, like the lizard,
our faces are heliotropes
or dog-daisies, opening like umbrellas
tracing the ups and downs,
reading hot cold wet dry;
the crystal hard-edge scent of snow;
the atmosphere's high pressure
beating a pulse against the skull
conducting migraine from its heights.
Hearts and ears the measure of acoustics,
our tongues taste acid electricity like lemon
on this visitation in a neon yellow orchard.
A mackerel sky augurs warm days
in which no grass will bend or rustle,
the first, desultory blowfly;
the first light plane of summer.

In the twilight before sunrise
I leant to ask a taxi-driver
what sort of day might follow
in the city to which I had just flown.
He replied that in his religion
it was a sin and went against the will
of God to look into the future.
I like to know what's around the corner,
to pre-empt surprises in the sky.
This could indicate a want of risk,
an inability to be mindful of the moment.

Forewarned was a crop saved on my parents' farm.
The weatherman was the oracle
before whom the family sat each night.

Reaching for another blanket in the dark,
pulling our knees close,
we are our earliest ancestors
looking out from hut and cave
to appraise the mood and shape of day,
the forces with and those to lean against,
the know-how of sun or rain on skin,
the solipsism of calm,
the continuum of change
since the dawn of civilisation —

Never mind Coriolis,
the effect of motion on a spinning body,
Earth's rotation on wind, ocean currents,
expansion of warm air.
Never mind that there is no such thing
as cold — just heat drawn away.

Dawn

Dawn finds its way into the house
through every recess,
projecting on to walls oblique
slow-motion shadow cinema:
toy canoe and sailing boat
navigate the bathroom wall;
a trompe l'oeil window onto moving trees
configures near a kitchen cabinet;
water in an unwashed bowl,
attuned to some vibration,
ripples across the ceiling;
a teaspoon on a sill glances ...
through cracks and keyholes, light
lets itself into the house,
not as a sly intruder
but with radiant in-pouring,
a casual, brilliant right of entry

Fayoum
Funeral Portraits of Roman Egypt

Funereal, it's two millennia of life
that so arrests. These individuals
are people I might pass out in the street:

priests, soldiers, children, women, men;
full gazes that reflect the inner self
like those of strangers that you meet

across a bus or train and fleetingly
in the unguarded moment see close up.
This woman circa AD seventy

with crow's wing brows, dark, languid lids and lips —
the disconsolate angle of her swan neck
calls attention to her sombre beauty.

Hauteur, assuredness, self-interest
emerge through worn-out caustic and gold leaf —
the lightest blush of hair under his nose

in *Portrait of a Youth*. Light silhouettes
the older man; the whites beneath his gaze
reflect — Christlike — the weight on one who knows

too much of life. The priest's an innocent
by contrast: slight of frame, young, lightly robed,
artless, nothing to declare, diffident;

the seven-pointed star above his brow
illuminates what looks like quizzical
surprise. In all, a solemn sentiment;

these portraits painted on the coffin wood
like missives from another age, are grave
and intimate. They make of time a sieve

and watch the promise and the pathos of
the passing days. As if they see behind
and what's before, they gaze with eyes that live.

Hierophant

The headlights strike and illuminate
for an instant a lone cow in a paddock,
like a thought lit upon and let go of,

an apparition in the vacuum,
solitary as the last man on Earth,
that eye, unblinking, in the blank night.

Not a sinuous gum tree, nor a row
of winter brambles to complicate
the emptiness. The cow's eye,

like an Egyptian cipher, caught
in the sweep of our brief passing;
all-seeing, devoid of censure, reproach.

Black Snake

We take it that the snake is mostly
with us now, tread carefully in long grass.

The garden has become subtler,
more interesting: sedge rustles

with a grey sagacity.
Grass skirts of agapanthus are dangerous.

The garden's slim black outlaw lends
a different complexion

to nasturtium and love-heart leaf
of violet. There is a complexity

to the wood-stack which has become
more than the sum of its parts,

the gestalt of negative spaces.
There is no longer just us and the birds

and the night-walking marsupials.
You cannot expect to meet it

Everywhere. Easier to believe in nothing
as your hand feels its way down the stem

of leek and spinach leaf.
Nothing's the dappled shade of dogwood,

musk leaf-litter under blackwood,
the seductive slot of dark beneath the shed.

The Nervous World

Just this: the green disc of the country showground,
a crowd's awareness shrunk to a sheepdog
and the vertical attitude of three Indian runner ducks.

Or to guessing the improbable weight
of an outlandish mandarin pumpkin
travelled in state at dawn on the back

of an old truck like a rotund emperor
or a courtly eunuch so much accustomed
to veneration. In the red and yellow

canvas booth, Punch, Lord of Misrule, continues
to kick over the traces and divide his audience;
the grey-blue hills of the tier are implacable.

In the rolling eye of the Belted Galloway,
who strains at his clove-hitched nose-ring,
the nervous world's mirrored.

To hold steady, here are the men in white singlets
sharpening the glistening steel teeth of their cross-saws;
the prize-winning and the non-prize-winning

cakes and preserves in the hall of industry;
the sheepdogs marshalling
nonplussed ducks: one, two, three, through a drainpipe.

Port

At Hobart's port, the past's tucked away
behind a tight veneer
of gallery, tapis, New Zealand possum
and Export Grande Merino.
Blue sky bounces off
the gloss white at the marina,
fishing boats squeeze into Constitution Dock,
Queen Victoria's renegade untouchables,
but there are rumours of new developments
at the freight wharves: fewer ships, the last train,
luxury accommodation
in the working warehouse.
Ghosts of canned jam and tomato
ride the conveyor belts through
five-star hotel and boutique aboriginal art.
At dawn, fishing trawlers tout their catch.
No rusting Japanese tubs alongside now:
shark-fins pegged along rigging
like ghastly washing lines.
Antarctic working ships zigzag
across the glassy wake of luxury liners.
Fairy lights are tinsel in the lime trees
all year round. The shadow of gas works
lies under a construction site; grain silos
entombed in river-view apartments.
Old Wapping's broken crockery and iron forks
scratch beneath the symphony orchestra
and international hotel.
An isthmus of clean sand and pebble

lies incognito under the jam factory
which is inside the school of art.
The mouth of the rivulet is a dry memory

of a time when it knew how to chart its own course.
History has been sand-blasted cleaner
than a free-stone quarry.
Everything rearranges: the cemetery
that was underneath the park,
the deep bush inside the graves,
the great blue gums that grew to the clear waters
of the river's broad plane ...
Industrial cranes, the overseers,
beckon sublimely to the future perfect.

Boy on the Roof, Wigan

Three storeys up, he braces
his feet against a clay chimneypot,
smokes a cigarette, exhales.

Contemplates this early Sunday morning
with a scowl which might just be a squint
against the brilliant sky or might

be the weight of that unadulterated blue
bearing down on questions
esoteric as a line of television aerials.

A few oblique metres away,
the skylight through which he has
just scrambled, is ajar.

On the ground floor a man
with tattooed abdomen stretches
and yawns. A woman at a different window

washes dishes in her nightie.
Trophies ornament the window sill.
The boy above their heads

looks out across miles of ridgeline
and terraced red brick like his own
to Tesco and BI-LO and Woolworths,

and three or four generations
grown out of the slagheaps
and belching chimneys of Orwell's Wigan.

He finishes his cigarette,
lies supine against the steep roof.
Arms folded across his bare chest,

face up to the astounding golden sun.

Tanker

The way that oil tanker seesaws
in the boiling mouth of the Tagus!

Slow motion was never so painful.
You could count to ten each time

it reaches equilibrium,
think the whole thing stable.

But fix your eye on the lumpy estimate
of the grey horizon then turn back

to the deck's distant platform
and you'll see the sliding forward

like a doomed ship,
prow submerging, the bell

of its ballast practically airborne.
Eternity ticks by before

the inexorable tipping back
through symmetry until now the stern

is sunk from sight,
the living image of catastrophe.

And the sailors out there
where ocean and river meet

riding the storeys of mountainous waves
up down like an elevator

today and tomorrow as the anchors drag
in the roar and din of the Atlantic –

are they afraid, or are they playing cards
as the pendulum swings?

Rowan

One thing is certain.

Though it is hard to say at what point
the sense of something impending

comes closest to breaking.

Starlings decorate the rowan tree
static as an illustration on a card,

one integer to each branch tip,

perched in hieroglyphic profile

against blue, white or grey sky,
imminence in stillness,

in the way each beak points southwest;
as if awaiting some apocalypse

[which might be Spring].

At a signal,
one or two birds change branches,

or fly off,

and then one or two
birds fly in from elsewhere
to take their places.

Sometimes the whole lot of them
lift off and reconfigure.

Again, a hiatus. The waiting.

Sometimes the whole lot of them

just up and fly away, leaving

the rowan, vacant, black
in its winter intricacy against the sky

(one branch wavering).

Sometimes, a single starling will remain:

the bird on the uppermost twig,

distilling anticipation

into its solitary profile

its seven note study.

Flood and the Woodman

Portent knocks at his heart
like massive river stones
rearranging in the night's flood.

The subterranean anvil of flux,
its volley and hammer
mumbling through the foundations

of his tin-roof house under the
butted hardwood floor, the iron bed.
Maelstrom is nothing new;

with every rain, the mountain stream
upends, uproarious,
flood its own stowaway

in sluice and spillage.
But tonight, this mute bass
in the marrow, of water rolling

rock on rock, like cracked bells,
this hubbub in his skull
augurs the unthinkable.

Freedom

Freedom walks across the road
like some triumphal flag
held aloft; the grey sans serif font on white,
a logo on an outsized shopping bag.

The swank and stride of future in another time
might have found its locus in a boar or bear
slung across a sharpened pike, a trophied ring
or seal; severed head of enemy; loot to share

the bounty of. Something runs deep
in the cut and thrust of acquisition. Glassed malls
are the new hunting grounds. Purchase ranks with sex and food.
Thrift's the black sheep on Consumer Street. Austerity appals.

Lake Pedder

Slower than a lunar tide
innocence began with water:
a mute creeping through granite sands,

the slow reticence of sedge and moss
to submit to their new element,
and the slower submission,
the slower, deeper reluctance of gum trees.

Against the convex arc of the dam,
with all the sullenness its nature could muster,
water's long bout of passive resistance began.

Grey Butcherbird

The one who inhabits the voice
of pure, fluted reason

is the one who carries the bill
with its lethal hook.

The bird whose song opens
in the day an idea of its own brilliance

is the one who'll ransack blind fledglings,
toss a nest distraught upon the ground.

The artless chorister is the same butcher
that hangs its twitching meat in fork of tree.

Joy's unfettered melody carrying through the bush
will clear the undergrowth of small birds in an instant.

Enrapt

The crescent moon and Venus
hang over the city tonight like lovers

as if the rest of the stars,
the galaxies in the background,
did not matter,
enrapt in their intimacy;

first to light up the evening sky,
already low in the west,
they will soon disappear behind
the mountain's deeper blackness

like a couple quietly absenting
themselves from the crowd.

Family Tree

You close your eyes against the light of day,
against the chaos which is frailty
and age; and seem to sleep, but answer in
a sound affirmative when I propose

to read the too-small print you've put aside.
The mantra of our DNA begins
in seventeen sixty five: *name, parents, place
and date of birth, church.*

Then *marriage, occupation* (mostly farms,
stonemasonry). Lastly, *date of death*
and *place of burial.* My finger trawls
the branches of the family tree:

the progeny of each new partnership
and those who died at birth or infancy.
I think perhaps you've drifted off
but once we near the twentieth century

with eyes still shut, you join the litany.
Behind closed lids, the living dead appear
in answer to their spoken names,
step forward one by one as if in light.

Outsiders

An immigrant family,
ours was a small island
on the island we had moved to.
We grew up watching our backs
and tending the votive fire
of our abandoned culture.
We liked English trees,
BBC TV and rain.
On Sundays we made forays
into the New World in the EK Holden,
compiled notes like Banks,
Labillardière and Darwin
on the flora and fauna
and, most copiously, the people.
Childhood was a taxonomy
of binary difference.
The youngest, I grew up taking notes.
At the Electrolytic Zinc Company
my father, scorned in the machine shop
for his white shirt and tie,
clung for dear life to his reference points,
gravitated to migrants like himself
and discovered, from this antipodean angle,
he had more than a little in common
with wartime Germans.
Outsiders posed a threat
to the island way of life.
You had to stick close, stand watch,
be careful not to leave the door ajar.

Darwin's Orchestra

The pause, adrift in space,
before the baton's swift descent,
its mark in time.

A moment since the tuning
and the static through millennia
from Neolithic skin and stone,

clay drum, grass reed and trumpet shell;
from air's vibration in the first bone flute
this arrow flew through its trajectory.

An evolution's labyrinth
that twisted, stalled at crossroads,
dinned with fire the casting and tempering

of bells and gongs and flared the horn,
conjured up the horse-tail bow
through riders in the Central Asian Steppes.

The odds as narrow as the fact
of our existence with its gravity and light,
its carbon and its air and life; the confluence

of craft and pitch, trained in the primal ear,
tuned in ancient Greece
to time's pure mathematics.

And in the hieroglyphs of scores
on music stands the history
of the enlivened mind,

its strenuous reach
through beauty's order and disorder,
its mayhem and its harmony.

That each step should lead, be led,
by chance and with such certainty
to this orchestral symphony,

as much a marvel as the physics of the eye
that sees and ear that hears;
this ephemeral deceit that flies
sublimely in the face of entropy.

Far and Near

Everything near becomes distant
— Goethe

These reading glasses highlight how the cost
of growing older is the detail that is lost
in the close-up. Some things I see anew.
Some skills I find again, like drawing a thread through
the eye of a fine needle or a louse
egg from a child's hair; the numerous
colours in the cat's fur when I thought
him uniformly grey. My eyes report
the clarity of daughters' eyes and skin,
the years which love for them have written in
their father's face as shadow.
Without the magnifying lenses though,
I take the fine print to the window sun
or hold the printed page at arm's length; on
this paper now, my writing tends to blur.

A process of inversion has occurred.
Somehow the distant has moved near:
the black-faced cuckoo shrike against the farthest tree;
once inaccessible lines of poetry.
Geography and history
mean so much more to me —
I want to know how people thought and slept
and lived in Rome and China and Egypt
a hundred or two thousand years ago.
Sappho, Rousseau, Michelangelo,

stone-age men, before words, how did they see
it all? And television's importunity
invites contemporary comparison –

the father sheltering his son from gun-
shot, old people ousted from their home:
they all become your uncles, parents, nieces,
or your cousins, not so many different pieces
but a whole. Through the long-range view,
even the planets take an altered hue
that seemed abstract, mere pinprick tricks of light;
like Saturn's ringed innocence at night.

Luck

My mother told me once —
she was seventy perhaps —
how, in the night from time to time,
my father took her hand
and that, in those moments
she reflected that she had been lucky
in life for all the pain it cast.
I think of them, like that,
in their house by the silent river,
side by side, holding hands,
the world and its great troubles
in the dark all around them.

Hens at the Water Bowl

The day is hot and I have thrown away
the water they have spoilt.
Now I stand to watch them drink
the clean fresh water from the bowl.
They dip their heads in synchrony then stretch
their beaks, like swans, toward the sky
to let the liquid trickle down their throats;
in all, a simple choreography.
They pause to revel in the luxury.
For a moment nothing is so beautiful
or calm as this hiatus. Side by side
the russet and the smoky hen,
statue-still, devotional, thirst slaked;
a clear ellipse of water, egg-shell blue.

Palliative

The guides are here now, your valets;
their government car is parking outside.
This is your street. This is your house.
These are your coronation flamingo path lights.
This is the gate with the difficult lock
that snags in the peach Cecil Brunner.
Here are the steps to the kettle that steams
and here, through its vapour, your view
of the broad, silver river mouth,
its widening plane, the ethereal, silvery hills.
Light glances from liquid amber and eucalypt leaf,
light from the water's widening plane.
The ushers have come knocking ...
But here are the books on the kitchen table,
here are the plates in the sink.
And look at the time on the starburst clock!
your children will be home soon.

Hay Load

Top-heavy, the load's balanced,
steady as a fat man on a stool,
each chopped stalk tucked, woven,
neat as a rush seat on a ladder-back.
Late summer hay, second crop,
the grass is hard baled, dense as fruitcake
drawing the eye from the flashcard
road-signs and the colour-blur race
of oncoming traffic passing
faster than a pulse; focus flickering
from speed dial to the parallel lines
of the road ahead which converge
and never converge. The hay truck
with its load is timeless, its order speaks of
seasons, atavistic labour, a job well done;
it stills my mind ... like the plumed rooster
scratching on the gravel shoulder of the highway.

Optics

Summer's drifting lazily into autumn,
days suspended breathless on a thread;

the dazzling decay of fig, grape, blackcurrant
beguiles our unreliable senses.

A column of gnats opens up the moment:
a hologram against the clear sky's void.

Close one eye and the swarm's subsumed
by the world of rank appearance:

a pumpkin vine on the move
up and over fences toward winter,

pears ripening to russet,
apples to red, yellow, green.

Through both eyes, the double helix comes to light again –
Plato's moving image of eternity –

spinning its intricate motion,
its vast, timeless, unceasing loop.

The Artist John Glover's Tomb

The terrier mutts risk throttling themselves,
coughing and gagging on the circumference
of link-chain tethers, tin bowls clattering
out of reach; they'd die of thirst or hunger
before passing up a pop-eyed opportunity
for strident polemic aimed at passing strangers.
On the periphery, the big black dog,
unchained, could teach the bellicose pair of them
a thing or two about hate and hot air. He stands
close to the wire as he can get, shows those
who leave their cars down at the dusty road
to read a few words on a stone, next door,
the malevolent reds of his throat,
his rancour belching from his barrel chest.

Old Roads

Old roads, byways,
wrap themselves around hillsides,
saunter along contours, acquiesce
to outcrops of quartz and dolerite.
Old roads skirt ironbark and blue gum,
zigzag down valley gradients
to wind unhurriedly up the other side.
History, myth and anecdote
stick to geography along old roads
like insects to tacky fly-strip.
Early road-maps were ribboned
inventories in calligraphic word
and pictogram
of all the traveller might encounter:
moor, marsh, gibbet, church,
alehouse and Dangerous Corner.
Old roads were unhurried,
blasé concerning detour;
came into being and went out
of their way to take water, trade
and the dead into their ambit.

I would not want this poem
to read as a litany of nostalgia,
I too mostly want to get
from A to B
and am not advocating
that theodolite and dynamite
be banned or damned

or that we trade routes
with number appellations
for lanes with names
of long-winded physiognomy;
that we reinstate cross-cultural
compounds and poetic imagery
out of some anachronistic need
to live life more slowly.

Where I live though, the DMR
is hell-bent on curtailing
serendipity and deviation.
A line is drawn
through thirty thousand years
of riverbank life: carbon relics
of old cooking fires. crustaceous meals,
remains of flinty cutting tool and spearhead.
Flyovers in steel and concrete
uphold the perpetual present
from which I'll turn off
and detour into the meandering past
to be reminded of how, on old roads,
you know the shape and texture of
the land you travel through.

The New World Book of Detail

The world map floats in a false blue present
of fixed littorals and politics

but the bee-boxes are abuzz —
June, July, the bees, too restless to sleep,
already busy with their waxworks.
Shift-workers, they have skipped a season

like the night-purple iris now unravelling
or the hen which has not paused in her laying
— scarcely a morning when the straw was bare —
black swans on the river, already trailing cygnets.
It's July though, not October!
Where has winter gone this year?

The bees are frenetic, tea tree in sticky bloom,
heather's carillon in shades of vermilion and pink;
leatherwood already loosening
confetti on to wild rivers.

On the beekeeper's bureau, the atlas
outlines continents and archipelagos in turquoise.
And islands, including that on which he lives,
a pink speck whose arrowhead points
towards Antarctica. The rest of the world map
is coloured in a water-wash pale blue.

Away from the bull's eyes of capitals
like Washington DC where cherries

are blossoming early; lesser towns
scatter in lower case. Behind small print,
more details come to light:

a shingle beach and water-play in place of ice,
the greater distance the guillemots must fly/
the polar bears swim;
glaciers melting out of slow time.

Inside a swarm's maelstrom,
the beekeeper, through clarity's fine-meshed veil,
forms a plan to shift his bees;
in future he'll follow winter
to higher altitudes.

Across continents and oceans and islands
the language of wide-range weather systems
is mostly generality.

In the New World Book of Detail,
a taxonomy of the particular might emerge:
the way a coral bed bleached of rose and peach blossom
resembles an evacuated city;
or how a desert without lizards is mind without thought.
Anyone might witness
the Sahara sands' ineluctable expansion,
sea water's luminous undermining of Greenland's shelf.

Replete, the honey-combs are dripping.
Between his thumb and index finger,
the beekeeper plucks a fallen bee
from the grass, returns it to the hive

of collective frenzy which is sweet, aromatic order;
wonders what the bees know of their future
and whether prescience measures the invisible
furthest from barn and hearth –
in the birds of the air, the scale and finned,
the brittle world of ant and beetle underneath his feet.

Shells

Between the hand-cream
and the Dettol
on the bathroom sill,
the seashells
that lit up on the shore like
works of ancient Moorish art,
still glistening
from receding tides,
are tawdry and seem to will
the household dust:
"Come, settle on us."
Chitons, agates,
paper nautilus
lifted from the coast,
the countryside
lose heart, become
so much ephemera.
Like sacred relics on display
inside museums, they shun
whatever quiddity
it was that gave them life.

Glass of Water

Bore water tastes of the grave,
smells of the gaze of an electric eel
cramped in its algal green
box underground aquarium.

Salt, void of enlivening air,
cataract or river motion;
for two million years this water
has lain below a vast continent.

To teeth and tongue
this viscous memory of ancient land
tastes of something
deeply, deeply sleeping.

Gulls

Did, somehow, the hill,
the shallow mud-flats and the current

of water conspire to form
a meandering vacuum

of passive resistance?
a safe haven for the gulls

this wild day in which the gale
is supreme commandant

lining up all things in its site:
fishing boats and leisure craft

at anchor, pennant leaves of gum trees
streaming like torrents of water

and roaring like water in flood,
even the Bolshevik sedge combs

horizontal, acquiescent.
On a day like today when the wind's

off-shore at seventy knots,
which qualifies as a gale

in a meteorologist's book:
a wind strong enough to lean on

at least, and to break like a pencil
a full-sized gum tree,

how does a host of hundreds of birds
on the bay, hold its own?

Does the hill with its forest crown
and farm-housed hem cradle them in its lee

on a ribbon of calm towards the further shore
where the gulls congregate like foam

or light on water between the waves
which race on either side

downstream and out to sea?
Or is their stillness an illusion

of the mess of white?
Now, narrowing your gaze you see

a single gull sucked swept flung
rent upwards and out of sight

while others struggle, dip and dive their way
back down to the flock's emollient white.

Two cupped hands of feather,
intention to the wind, bones light as air;

each bird threading beak and will
through the wind's great wall.

Anachronisms

1.

Stopping for cows in the twenty-first century
– all that mud!

the nap in the hide
like a wind-blown grass paddock.

Waylaid from your destination
by the slowness of towering beasts,

their hot snorts of disparagement
through a wound-down car window

2.

A cock crow in Erskineville –

cutting through the arc of a 747's
ascent in a blue sky over Sydney

3.

The soloist's shadow –
the page-turner,

making an art of old-fashioned effacement,
belonging entirely to another time;

eyes levelled to each note on the stave,
the page's dog-ear between finger and thumb;

arriving and departing in black
so discreetly after the pianist

and the applause,
that you might almost miss them

4.

On a wild antipodean mountain
at a eucalypt-pungent fork in the track,

an Italian violin-maker,
from Stradivarius' home town,

whose hands know the art
of coaxing melody from wood and gut

5.

The smell of rain on a child's hair,
earthy as a wallaby, a hot stable

6.

Sometimes slicing carrot, onion, parsley
with a sharp steel blade seems out of date;

fingers spattered with potato starch
seem like an error in history's computing

7.

Candid corpses of animals,
naked of fleece, hide, bristle
hanging by hooks through sinewy heels
in butchers' windows

8.

Milk,
newspapers
delivered to the door

9.

Handwriting in the letterbox,
the voyage of the envelope
from someone to you

10.

Postage stamps – exotic and mundane

11.

Finials:
the curly whimsical embellishment
to pediment or apex of a roof,

or the tapering needle on a gabled house
linking ether and earth in domestic life

12.

Churches. The musty, quietening smell of still air
conducive to private and communal contemplation

13.

– the word prayer. And sacred.

14.

Smokers in malls, the new pariahs,
and parents at traffic lights puffing fags

in cars full of kids, who, buckled in tight
gaze at the future as if through a rising tide

15.

Candles' passive resistance

16.

The click and slam of a car door,
its combustion engine's ignition *kakakacha*
sounding in the prescience of night, already obsolete

Cows at Night

Tonight, a herd of Frisians
tearing and chewing grass
leaves off being sound,
becomes sensation.

Our forebears, huntsmen and herdsmen
out on the Steppes, the savannah,
might, like me, have listened to beasts feed
in the dark of night's synaesthesia,

each blade rending and snapping
against the sod; sound, skin,
the gradient of the earth,
the depth of night, all one.

Sleep

Docile as lambs in the paddock,
passive as hens at nightfall
we lie down in the dark,
submit, like obedient children
to oblivion. Each night, this
practising the aloneness of coffins,
the blindness and blackness
and brief ignition of the senses
before we go: the click of a light-
switch like a gunshot;
letting go the homily
of skin and bone and viscera.
The dumb humility, the angelicness,
this nightly disrobing of the self.

Acknowledgements

Some of these poems have appeared in the pages of the *Age, Island, The Best Australian Poems* 2011 and 2012 and *Australian Poetry Journal.* The poems "Dawn" and "Enrapt" have been set to music for soprano and piano by UK composer Anthony Gilbert as part of a suite called *Peace Notes* (University of York Music Press 2011).

Grateful acknowledgement is made to the Literature Board of the Australia Council for an Established Writers grant and to St Michael's Collegiate, Hobart for leave which enabled the completion of this book. Arts Tasmania supported my attendance at the Down Under Conference held by the Faculty of Letters at the University of Lisbon in 2011, as a result of which some of the poems in this book were written.

Thank you to Richard Fogg and Margaret Day for "River Fisher" and "Twenty-first Century Skies" and to the book *John Glover and the Colonial Picturesque* by David Hansen for reference to John Glover's life and paintings. "[T]he slagheaps and belching chimneys" is a phrase from George Orwell's *The Road to Wigan Pier.* Thanks to Gordon Harrison-Williams for invaluable assistance with production, to Stephen Edgar for proofreading and to my publisher, David Musgrave at Puncher & Wattmann.

The epigraphs by Saint Augustine are from *Confessions Book 11* and by Stephen Hawkins from *A Brief History of Time.*

About the Author

Sarah Day lives in Tasmania. She emigrated from England to Australia with her family as a child. Awards for her work include the Anne Elder, the Queensland Premier's Award and the University of Melbourne Wesley Michel Wright Prize. *The Ship* was joint winner of the ACT Award. Her books have also been short-listed for the NSW Premier's and the CJ Dennis awards. Her *New & Selected Poems* (Arc UK) received a UK Poetry Society special commendation. She has been a member of the Literature Board of the Australia Council and was Poetry Editor of *Island* for seven years. She lives with her family in Hobart where she teaches Creative Writing and English as a Second Language to year twelve students.

www.ingramcontent.com/pod-product-compliance
Lightning Source LLC
Chambersburg PA
CBHW030854090426
42737CB00009B/1223